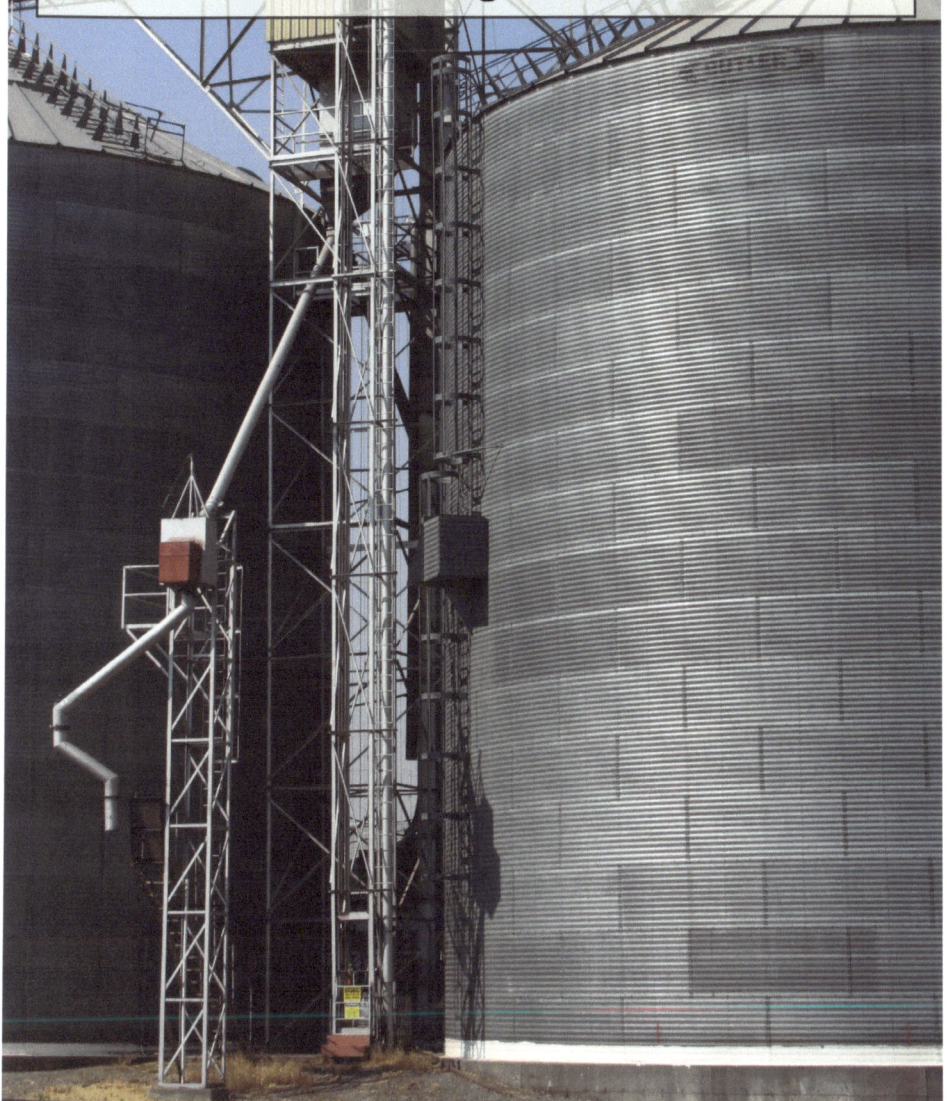

A Mark Dahle Portfolio

Monkey Brains
On Big River

Little Gibbon's Big Adventures #1

This is the first story about a gibbon who liked adventures. All the other gibbons called him Monkey Brains.

Books in this series include:
1. Monkey Brains On Big River
2. Monkey Brains On Big Ocean
3. Monkey Brains On Big Mountain
4. Monkey Brains In Big Desert

~ ~ ~

Mark Dahle Portfolios can be read in a few minutes and enjoyed for a lifetime.

Unlike many picture books, the text in this book is not related to the art. This might seem weird at first. One thing that makes it better is to order more portfolios until you get used to it. Fortunately, space is provided on the pages for you to draw your own pictures of Big River and Little Gibbon if you like.

This portfolio includes a beautiful 36 x 24 inch painting (at the right), twenty-six great photos from Spokane and Eastern Washington, and a story about an adventurer who called himself Little Gibbon.

Photographs in this book are available in limited editions. See http://www.MarkDahle.com for more information and for previews of upcoming portfolios.

We do our best to create portfolios free of editing mistakes. But it's hard to catch everything. We reward people who report errors in any Mark Dahle portfolio. For details see MarkDahle.com/Typos.html or email MarkDahle@aol.com with the subject line "Typos." Thanks!

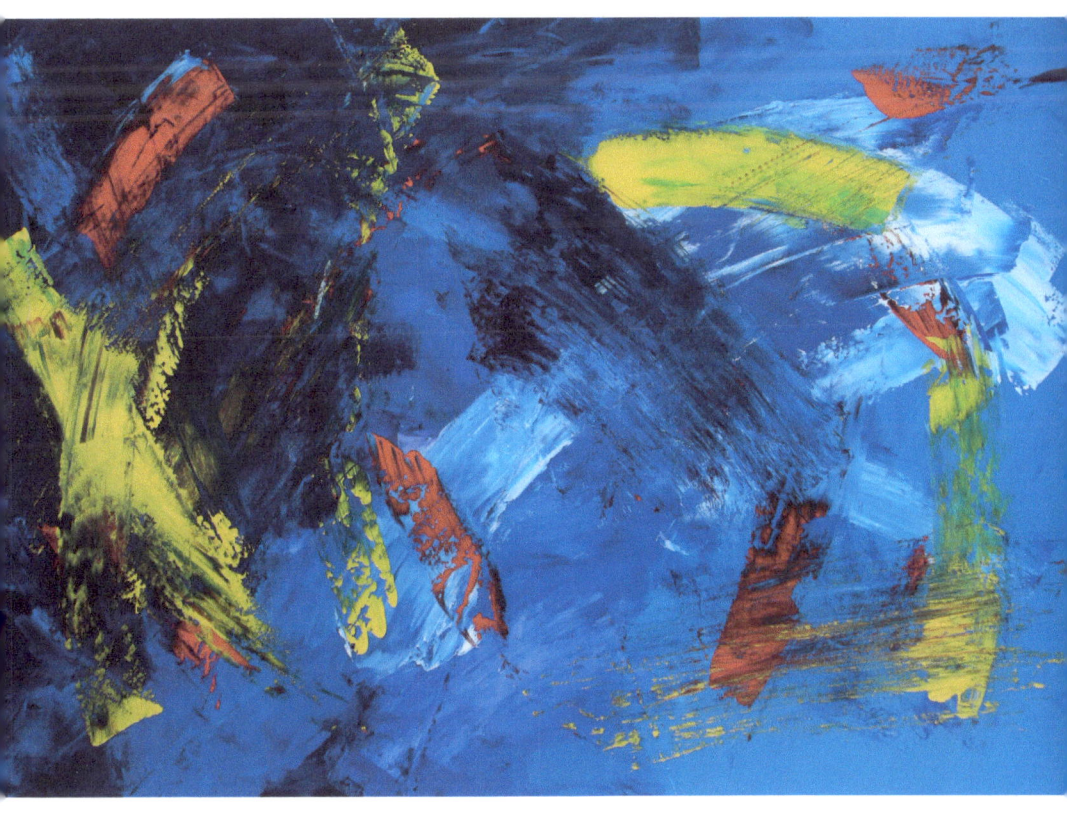

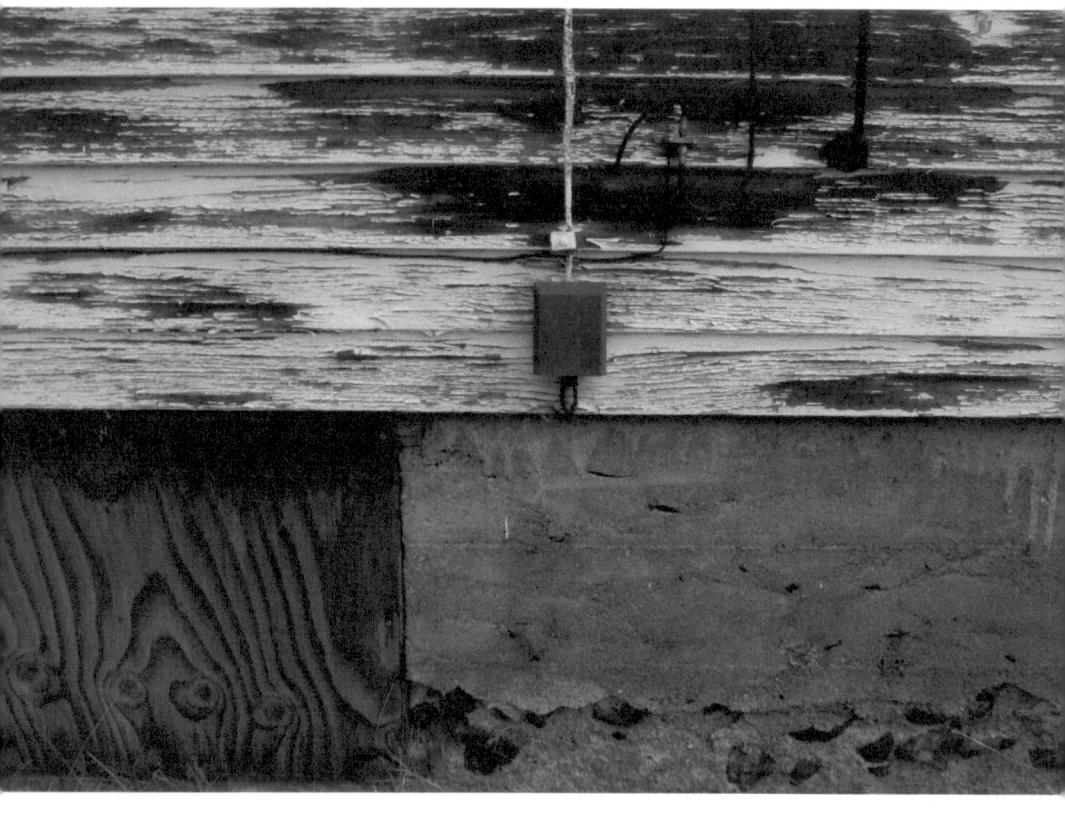

Gibbons usually like to swing from tree to tree. But the youngest gibbon in one family preferred adventures instead. He would swing in trees if it would get him to a new adventure. Otherwise he wasn't interested. As a result, all the gibbons he knew called him Monkey Brains. He called himself Little Gibbon, since he was still growing and learning lots.

One morning Little Gibbon picked Big River as the place for his next adventure.

He got his canoe ready and pushed off with one foot. His boot got stuck in the mud, and suddenly he had one boot instead of two.

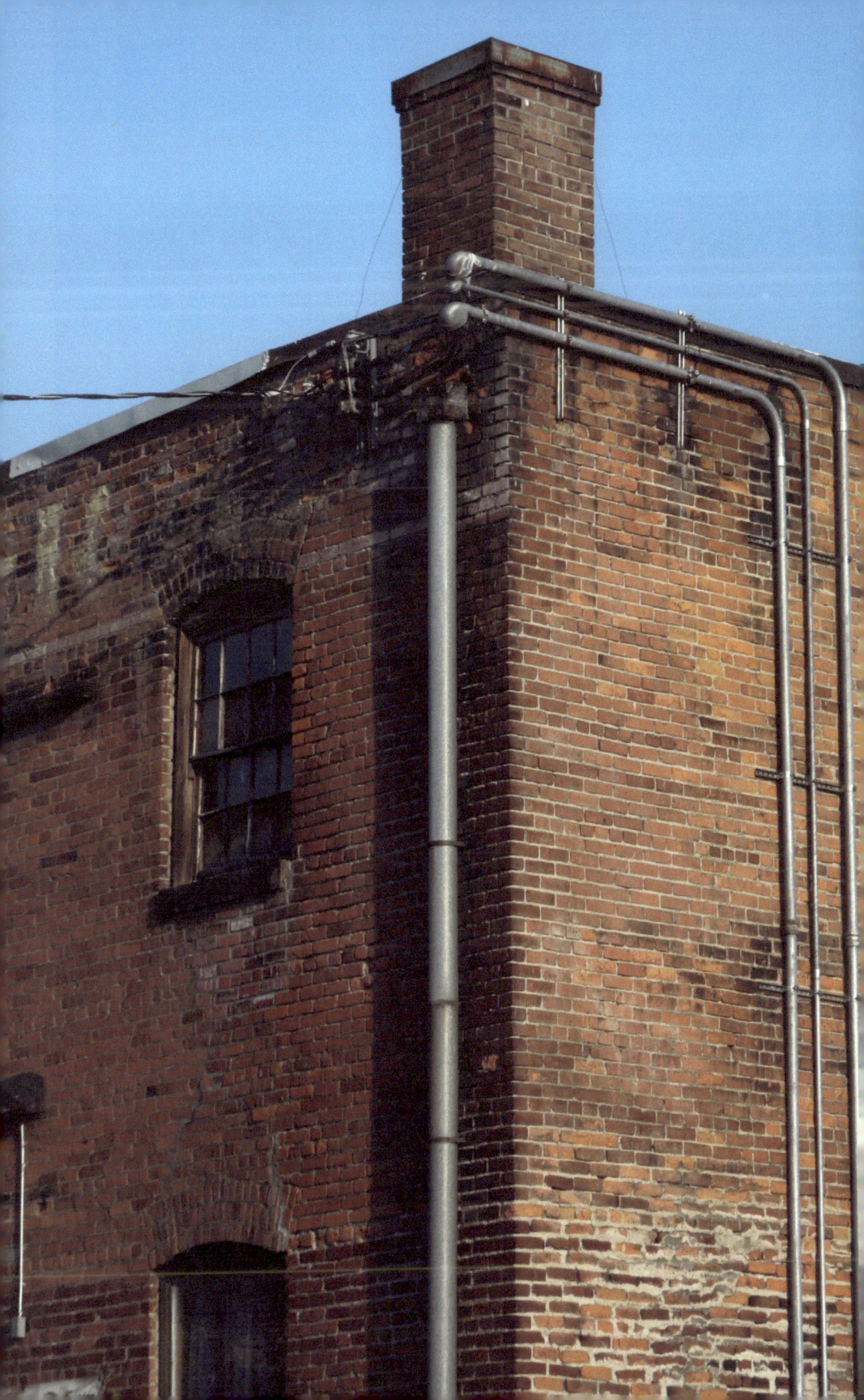

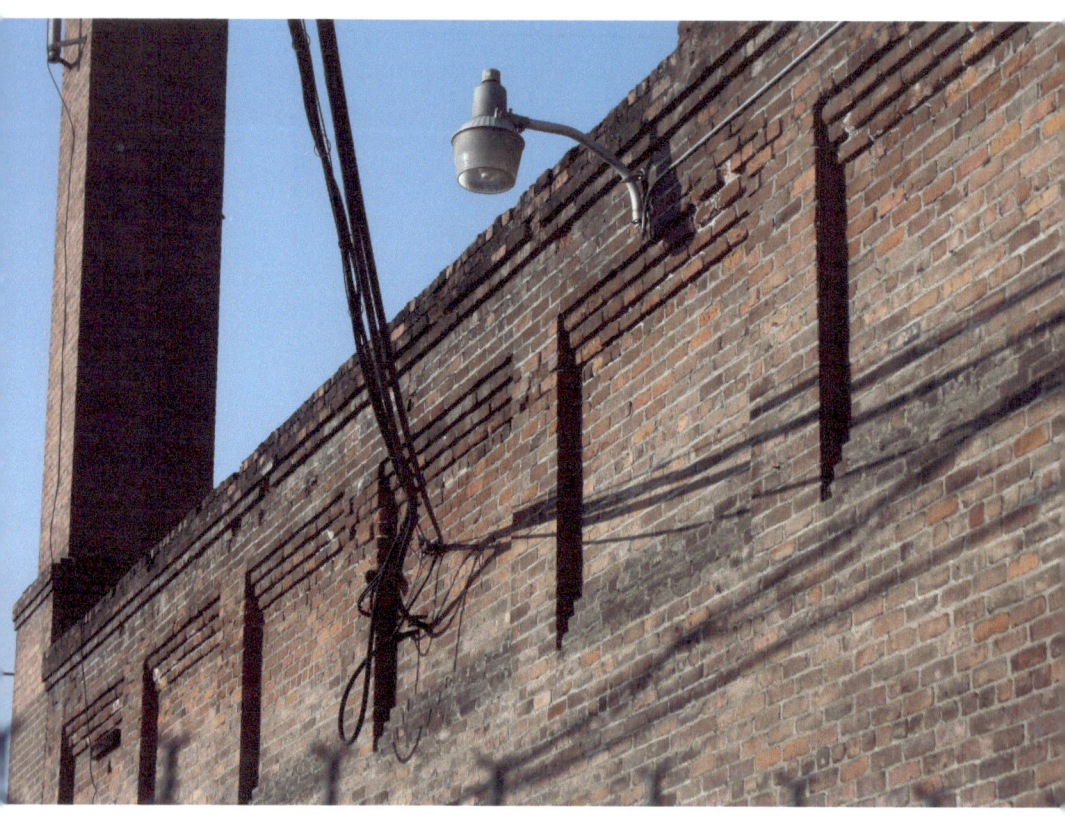

As he floated down the river, Little Gibbon could see his boot stuck in the mud near the paddle he had forgotten. But he was going on an adventure and he didn't care. Who needs a boot and a paddle when you want to have an adventure?

Luckily for Little Gibbon, Big River was in a good mood.

Six months earlier Big River had been swollen and cranky, in a terrible mood at every turn, but that was over. Now Big River was as calm as he ever got. There was very little danger except for the Bend With Big Rocks. At the Bend With Big Rocks, canoes often got turned around and stuck.

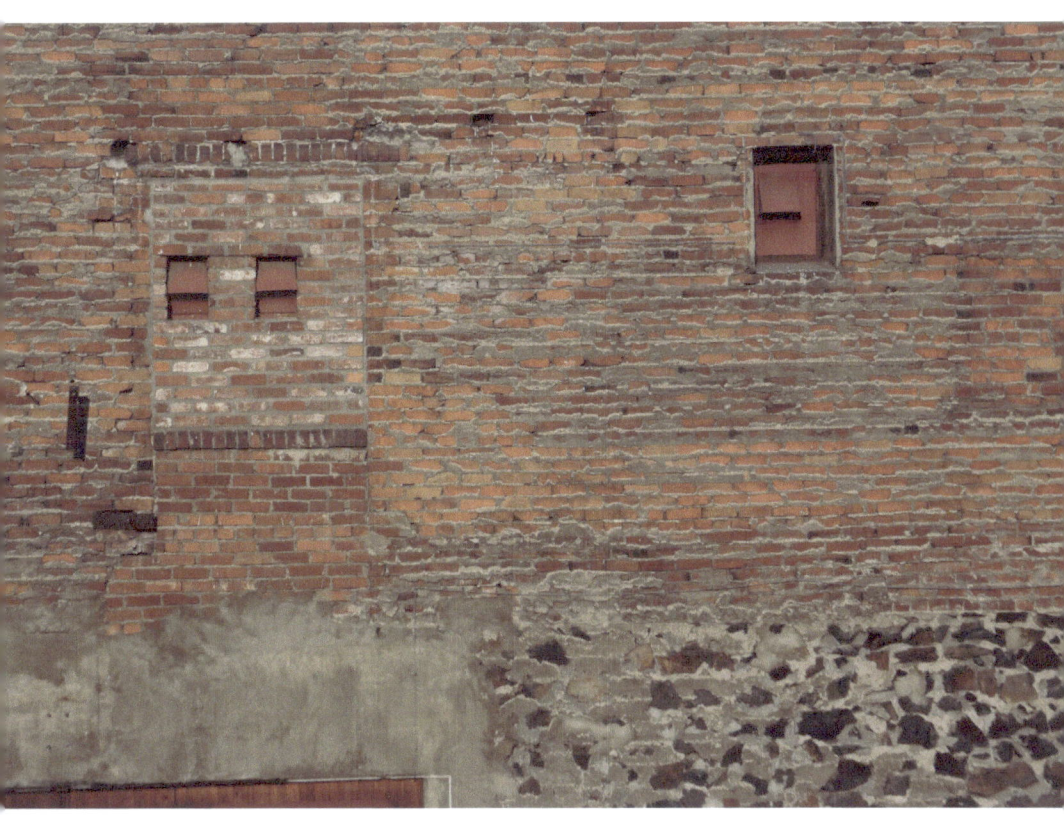

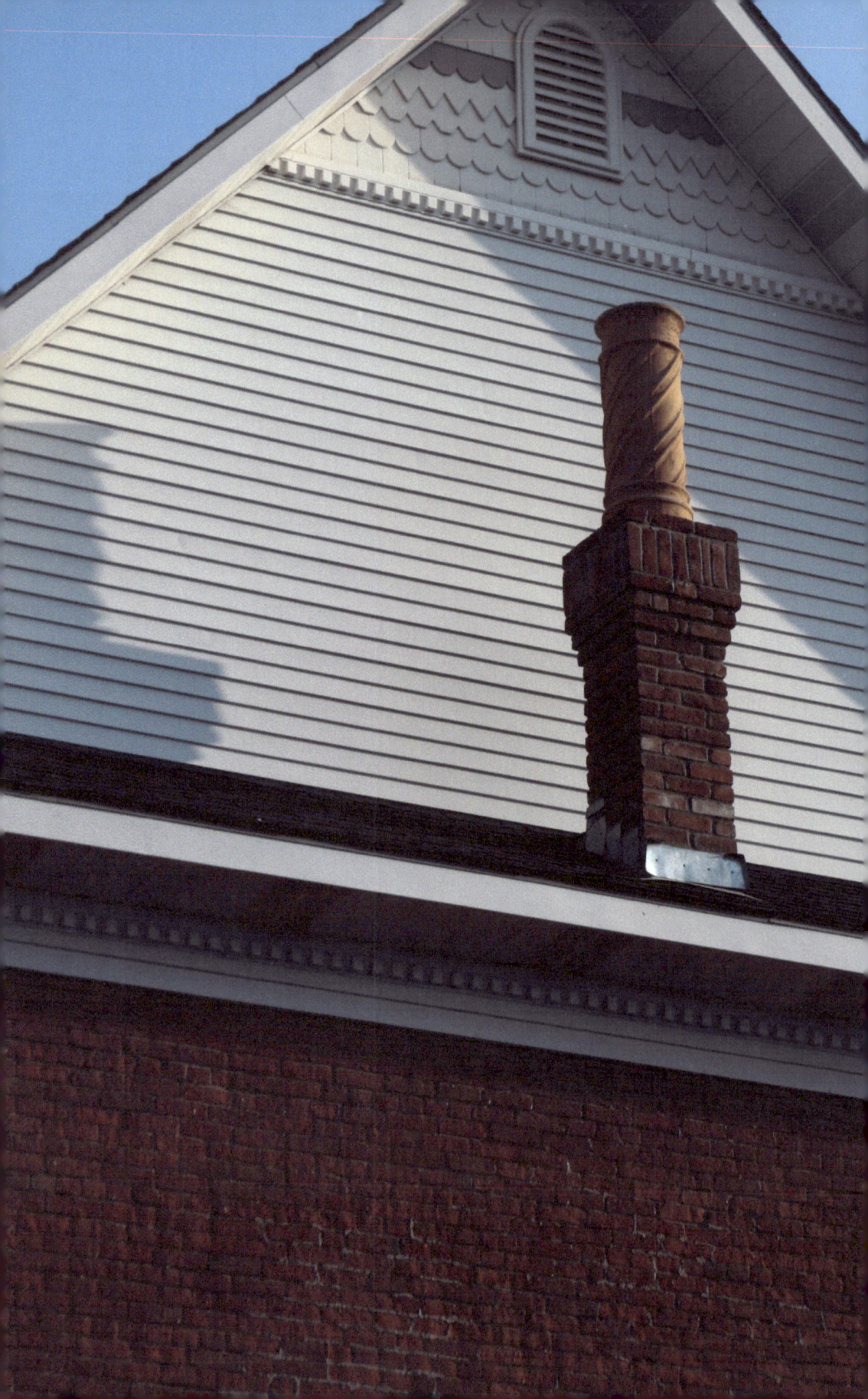

Little Gibbon looked to see what was ahead. He saw a bend in the river filled with rocks. Big rocks.

Little Gibbon smiled. "Big River!" he shouted. "We're going to have an adventure!"

Big River smiled and held his breath. He liked Little Gibbon because he never knew what would happen when Little Gibbon was around.

If Little Gibbon had brought a paddle, he would have been able to get through the bend without too much trouble. But the paddle was back near his left boot.

BAM! Little Gibbon's canoe slammed into the first rock.

BAM! His canoe slammed into the second rock and spun around backwards.

BAM! His canoe slammed into the third rock and got stuck.

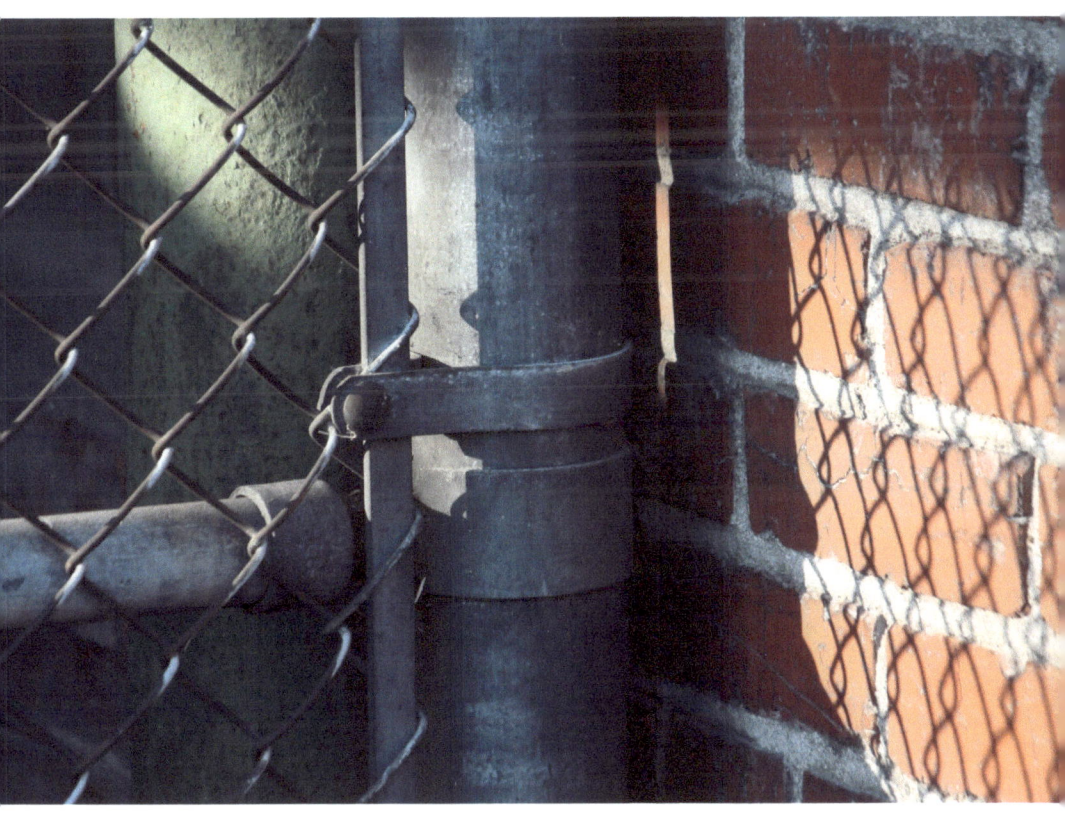

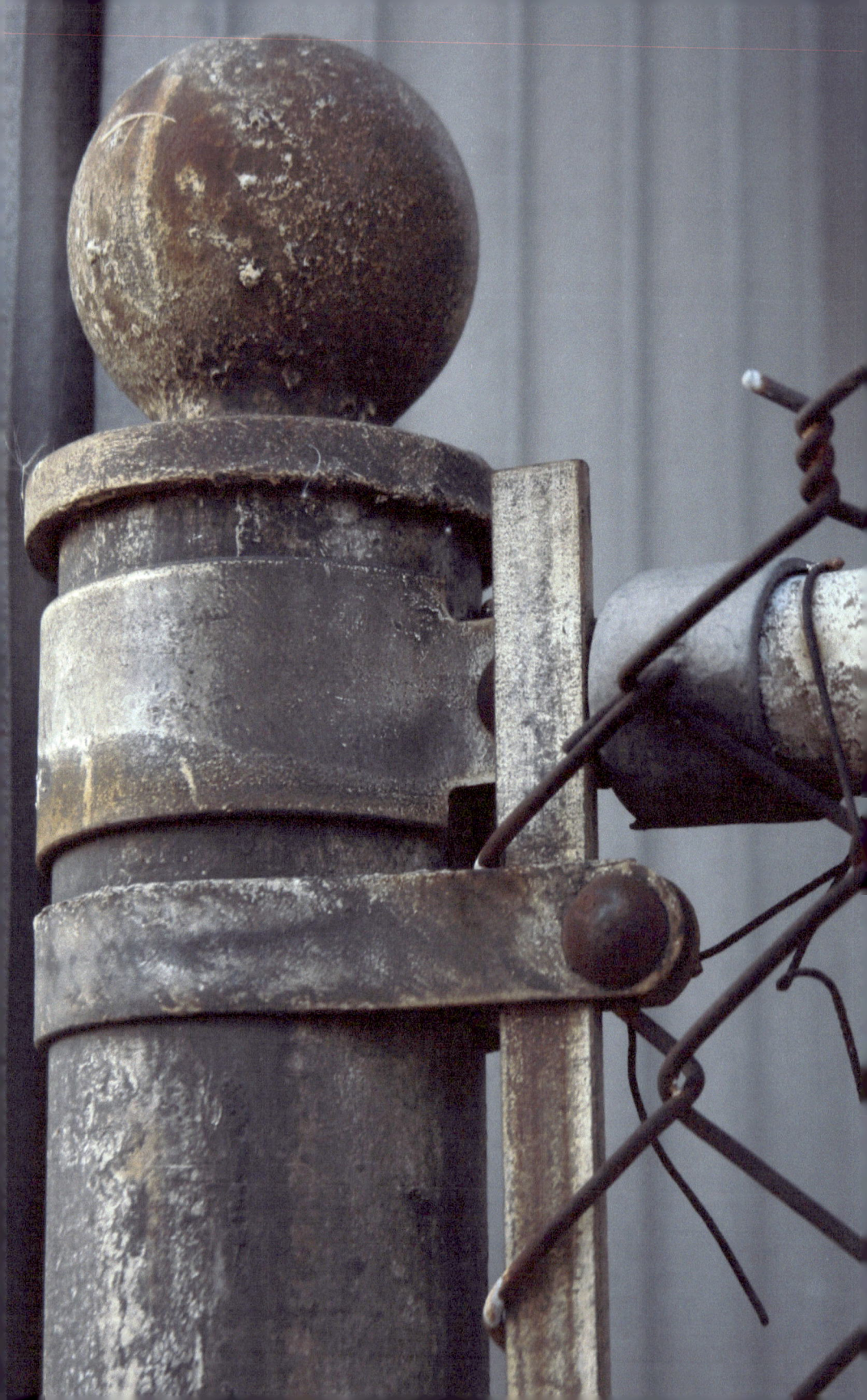

Little Gibbon pushed with all his strength and got loose. Now he was floating down Big River backwards.

"Big River!" Little Gibbon shouted happily. "We're having an adventure!"

When Little Gibbon reached a sandbar he stopped to rest. He took off his raincoat because it was so hot and put it on the sandbar. He turned the canoe around so he could see where he was going when he started out again. Then Little Gibbon got back in his canoe and pushed off with his right foot.

This time his right boot got stuck. When Little Gibbon looked back he could see his boot near where he had forgotten his raincoat. Little Gibbon didn't mind. You probably know why.

"Big River!" Little Gibbon shouted. "We're having an adventure!"

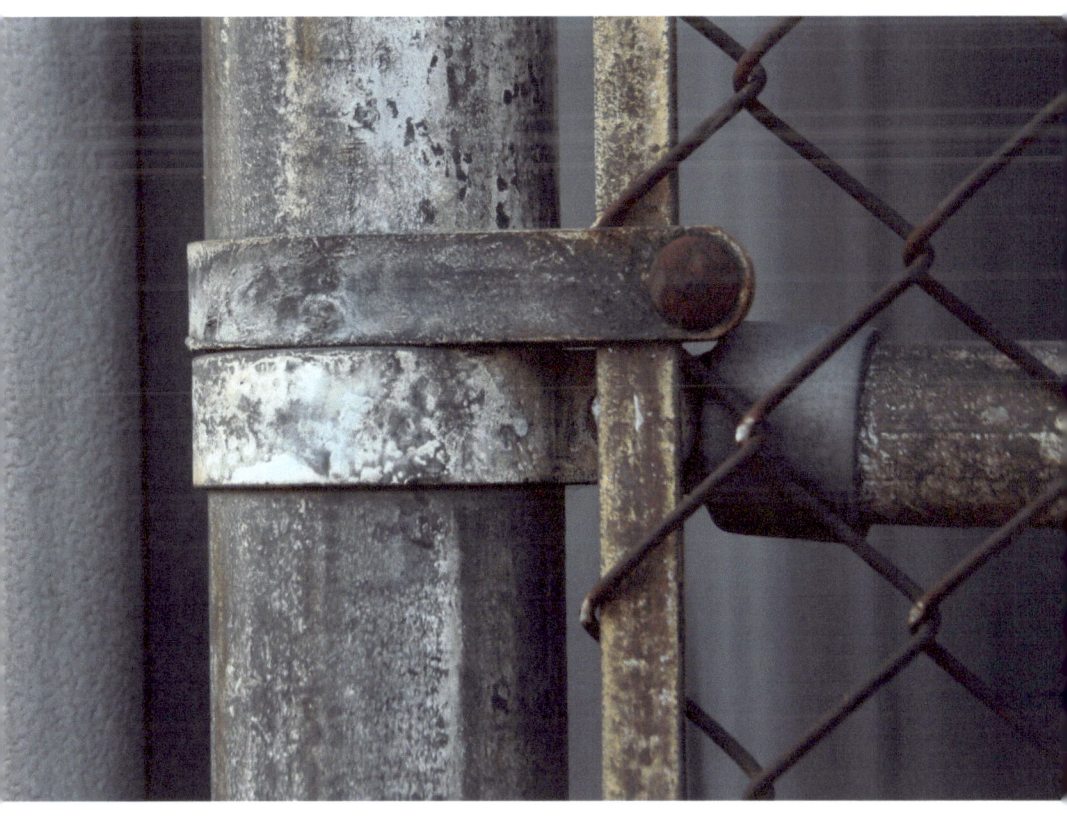

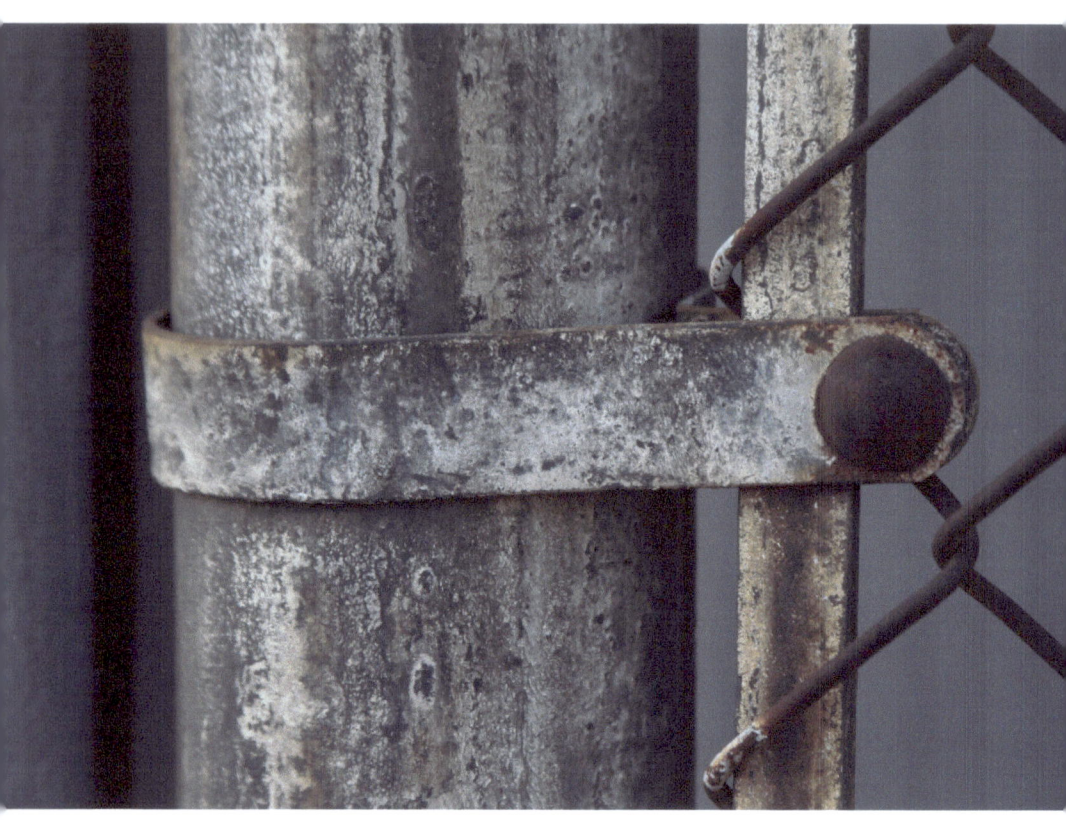

Big River sighed. He *thought* things would be better for Little Gibbon, now that Little Gibbon was past the Bend With Big Rocks. The rest of the river was calm and peaceful and posed no real danger, except for the Long Stretch With Fallen Tree Snags.

Little Gibbon looked ahead to see what was coming up and saw a place where the banks had collapsed and several trees had fallen into the water. He smiled. He was having an adventure.

If Little Gibbon had a paddle, he could have avoided most of the trouble with the tree snags. But without a paddle to guide the canoe, Little Gibbon kept getting too close to the tree snags and the branches of the trees kept poking him. He wished he had his raincoat. He had to duck several times (once he wasn't fast enough) and he got poked and scraped quite a few times.

"Ouch," said Little Gibbon. More than once. But he was happy. You probably know why.

"Big River!" Little Gibbon shouted with delight. Maybe you can shout it with him. "We're having an adventure!"

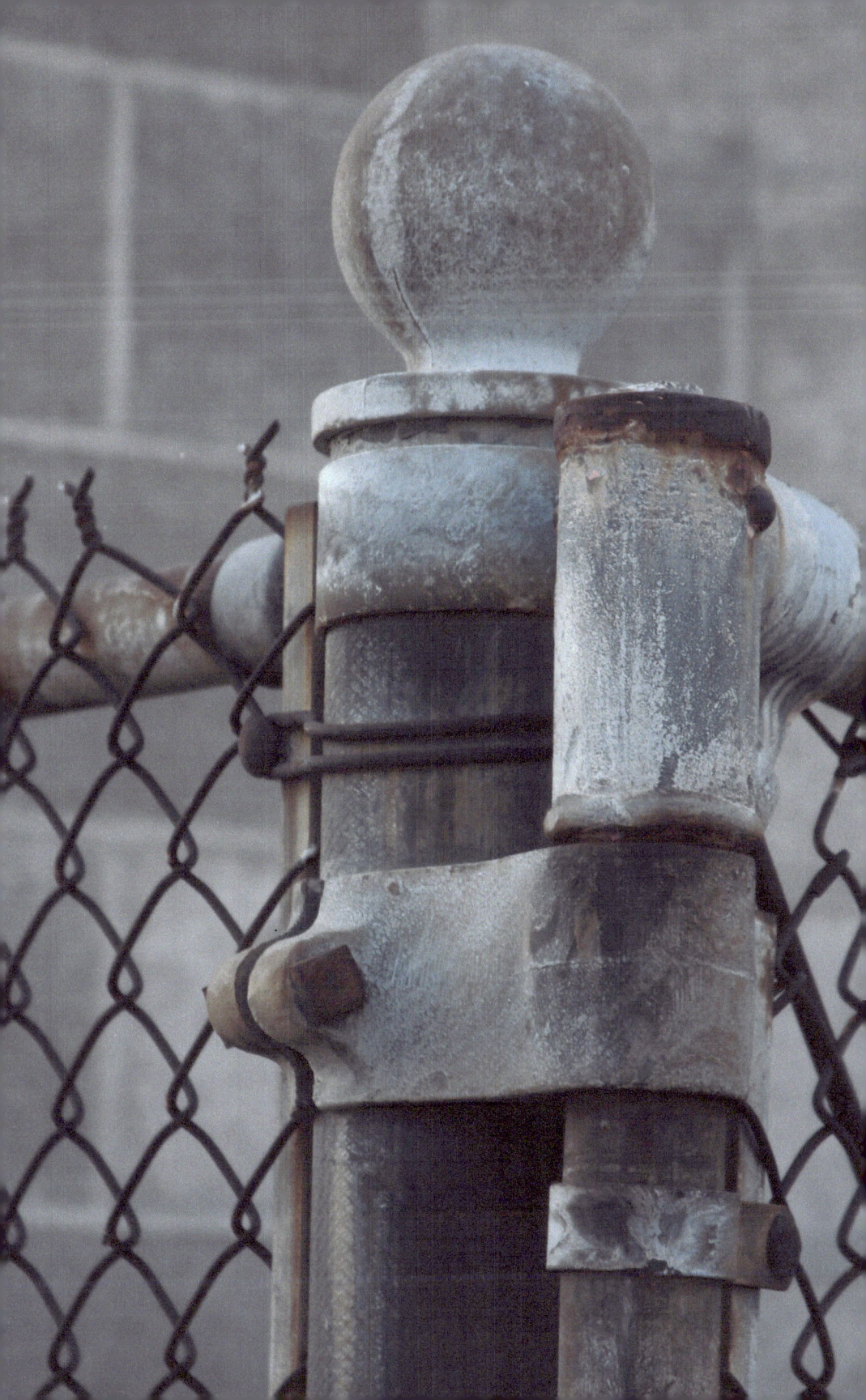

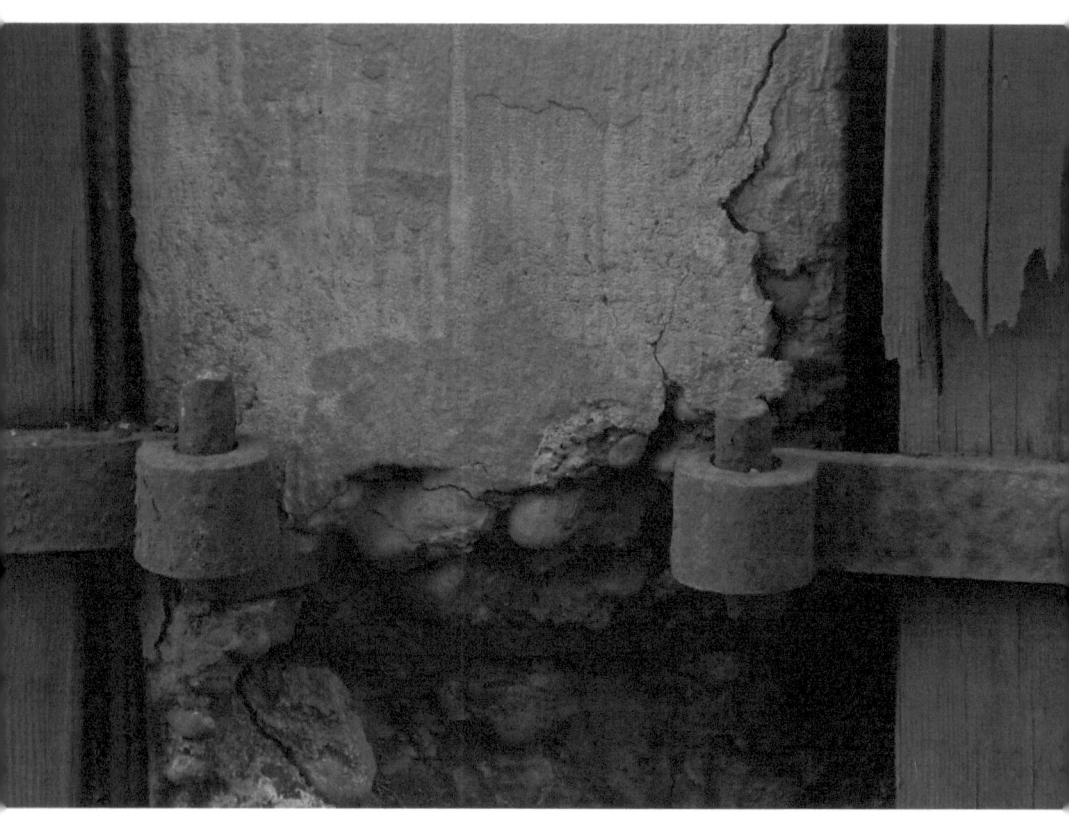

Big River sighed as Little Gibbon cleared the last of the tree snags. He *thought* things would be better for Little Gibbon, now that he was past the Bend With Big Rocks and the Stretch With Fallen Tree Snags. As long as Little Gibbon stayed in his canoe, there was not really that much danger from the Big Bumpy Falls.

"Big River!" Little Gibbon shouted. "I'm getting out of my canoe to go swimming!" He jumped out of the canoe and looked ahead. It looked like there might be some bumps in the river coming up, but he couldn't tell for sure because the river looked like it disappeared.

"Aaaaaah!" shouted Little Gibbon happily as he hit the first bump.

"Aaaaaah!" shouted Little Gibbon contentedly as he hit the second bump.

"Aaa (glub)!" shouted Little Gibbon as he hit the third bump and got a big mouthful of water. Then he went over the first falls.

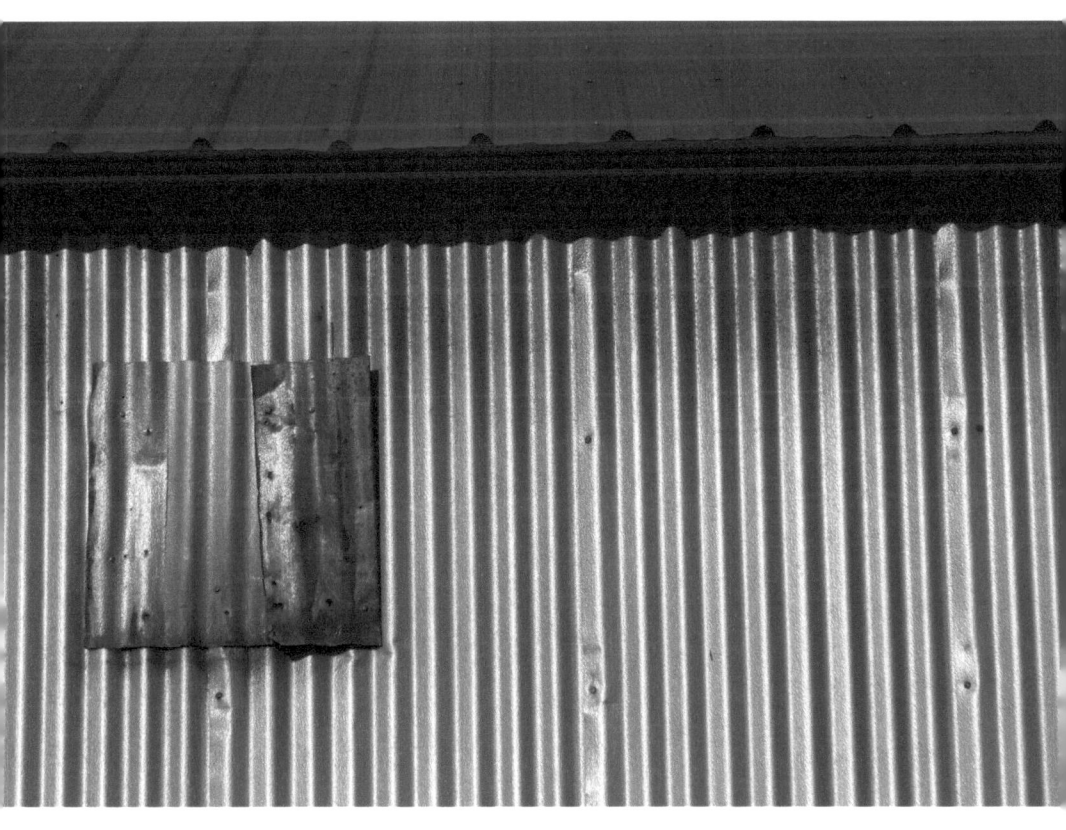

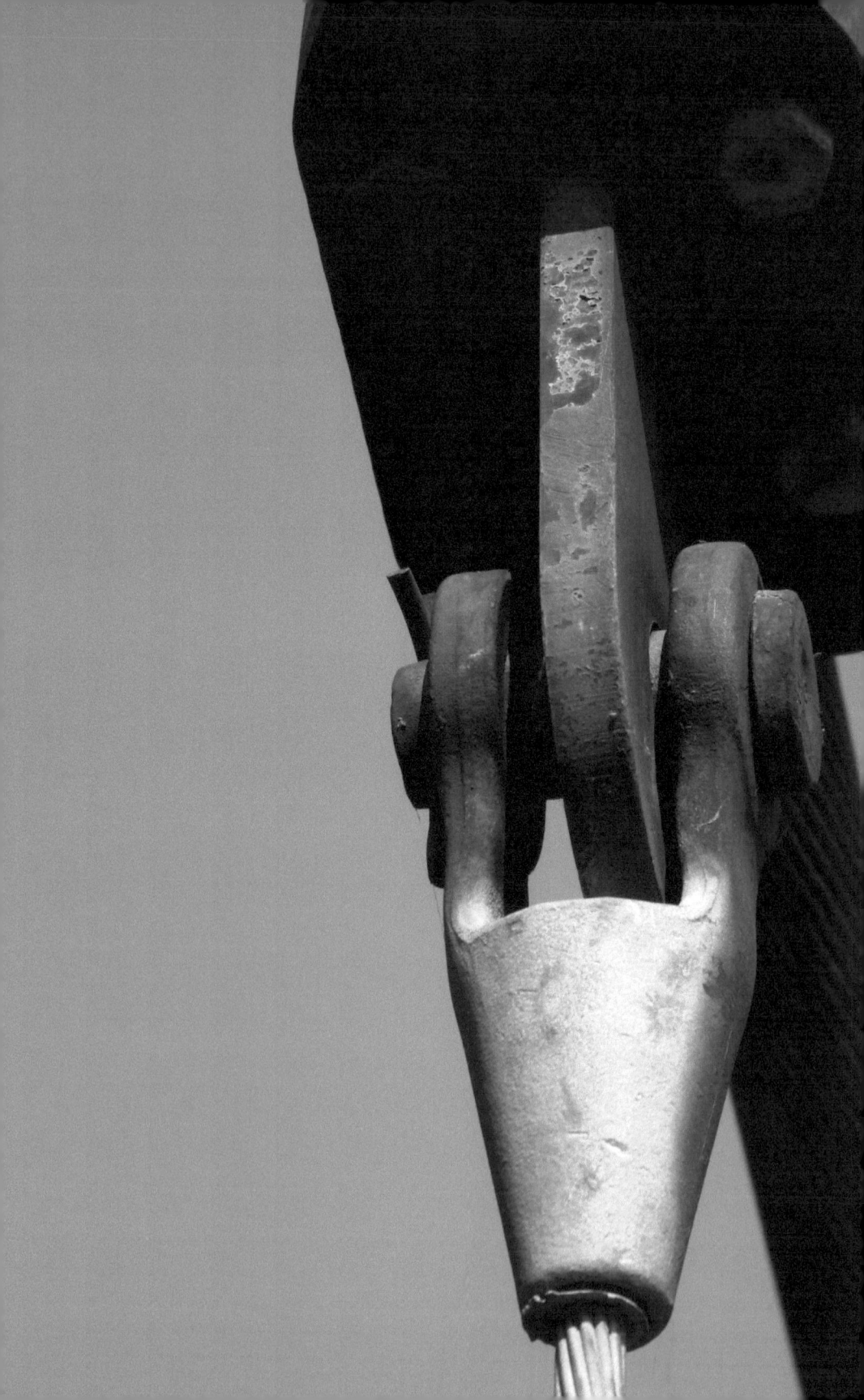

The first falls was five feet straight down, and Little Gibbon laughed with excitement because he was having an adventure and he could hear a bigger falls coming up. Up ahead he thought he also saw more bumps.

"Aaaaaah!" shouted Little Gibbon with pleasure as he hit a much bigger bump than he had been on before.

"Aaaaaah!" shouted Little Gibbon with wonder as he hit an even bigger bump.

"Aaa (glub)!" shouted Little Gibbon as he hit the biggest bump of all and got a big mouthful of water just as he went over the second falls – thirty feet straight down into a big churning patch of water.

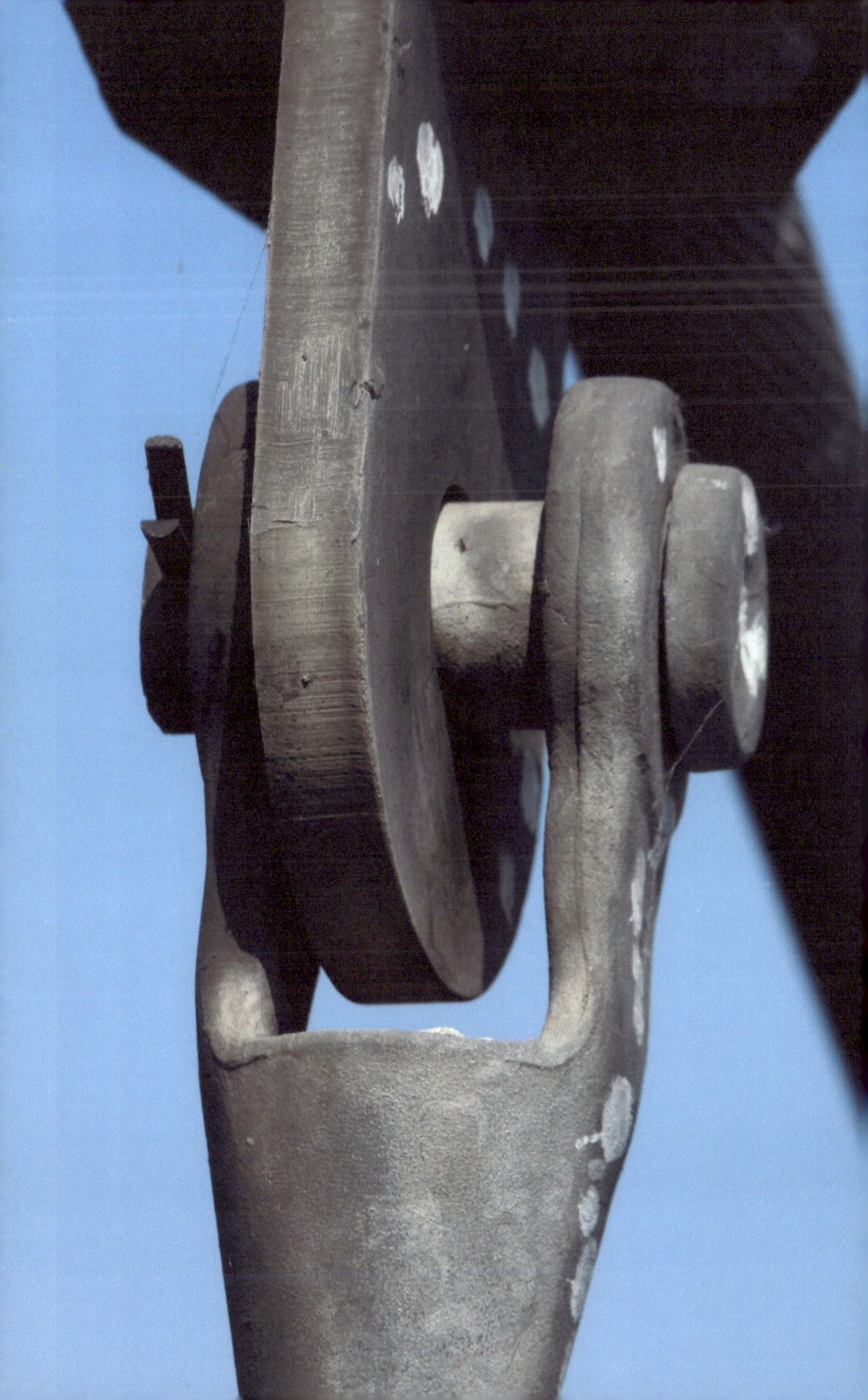

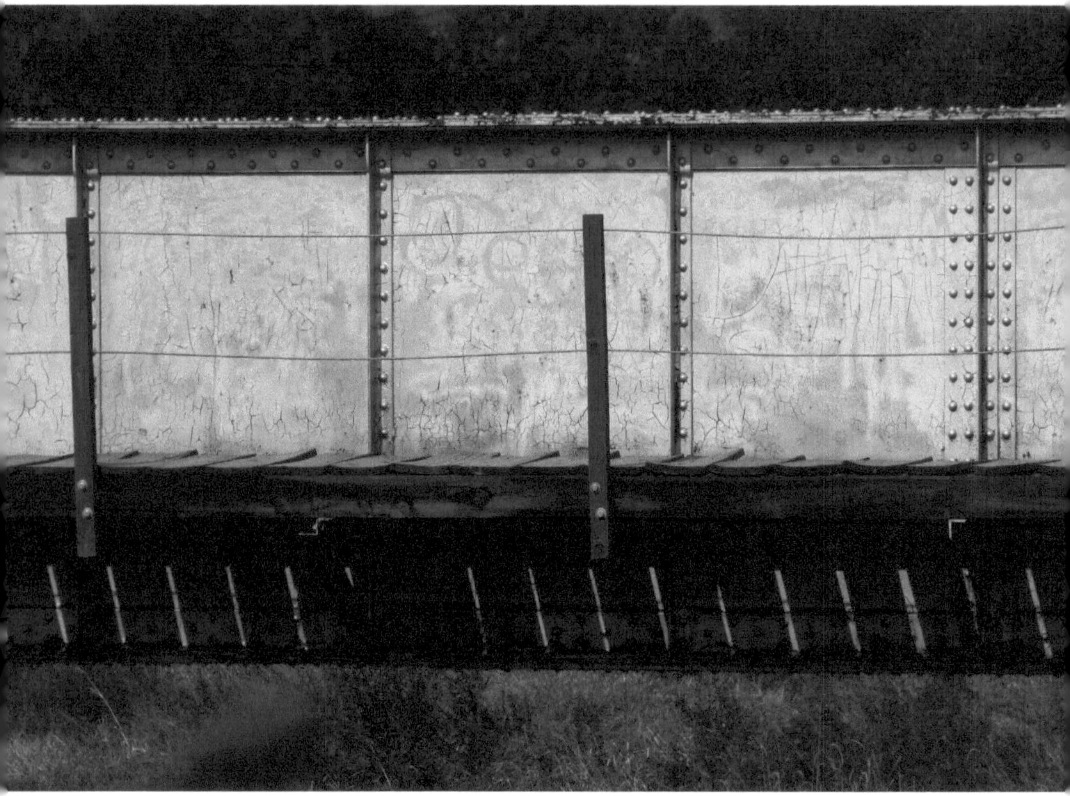

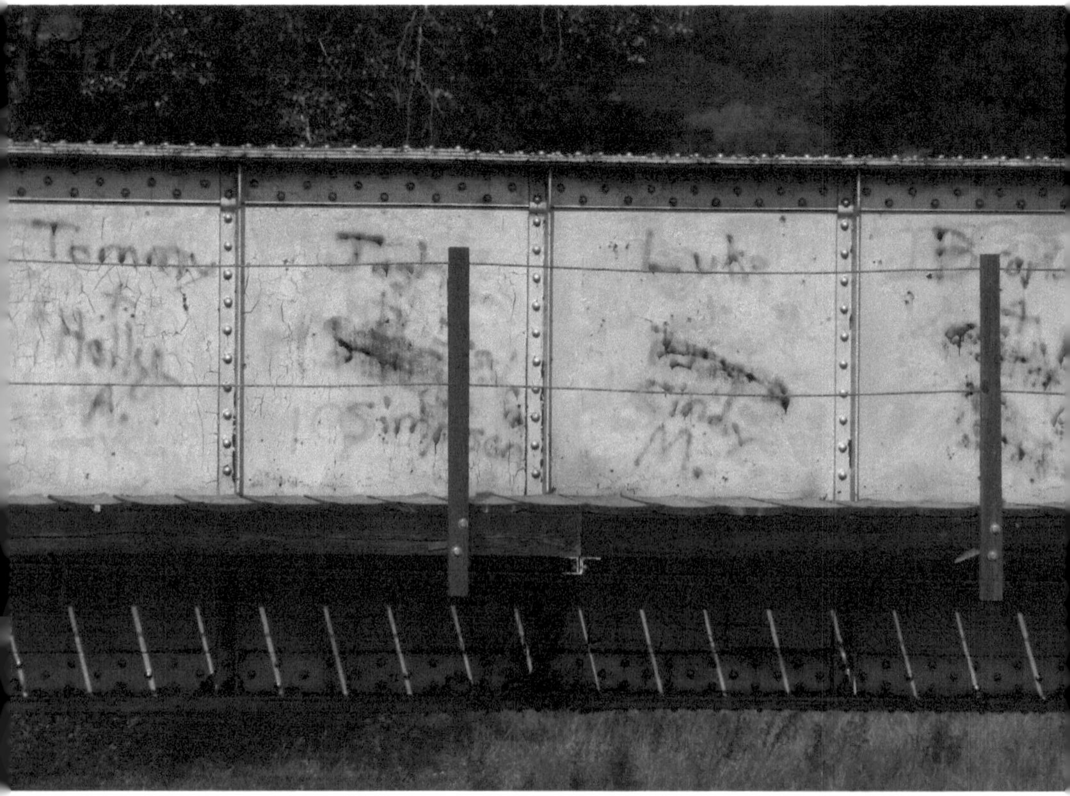

Little Gibbon was underwater for some time before he got safely to shore. The second falls was not quite as much fun as the first.

"Big River!" Little Gibbon sputtered when he was back on land. "That's almost *too much* of an adventure!"

Big River was relieved that Little Gibbon had gotten through the falls. There was almost no danger now that Little Gibbon was safely past the Bend With Big Rocks and the Stretch With Fallen Tree Snags and Big Bumpy Falls. About the only thing that could go wrong was if Little Gibbon fell asleep on the Island Overrun With Crocodiles.

"Big River!" Little Gibbon shouted. "That's enough adventure for today. I'm going to take a nap on that nice island I see up ahead."

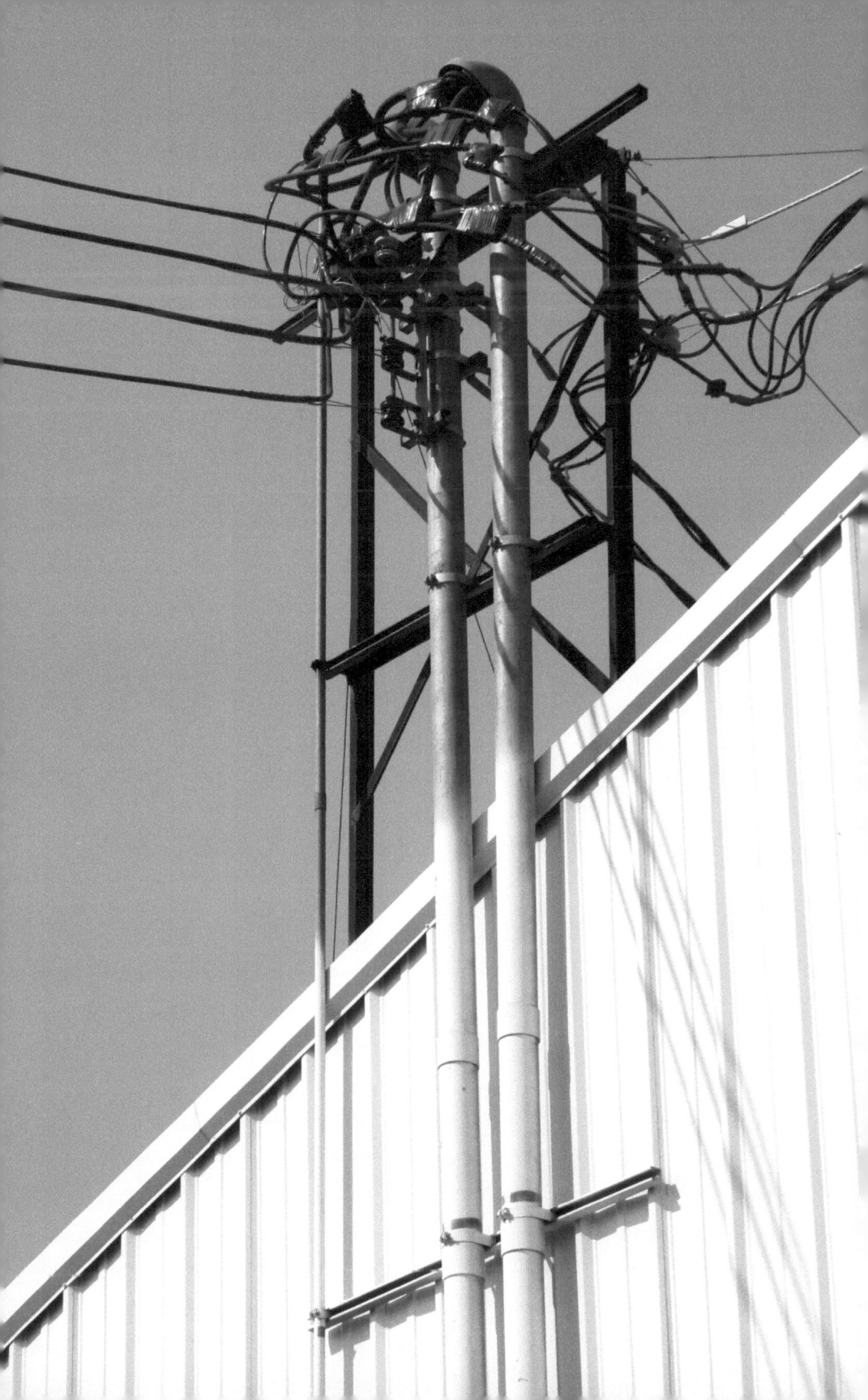

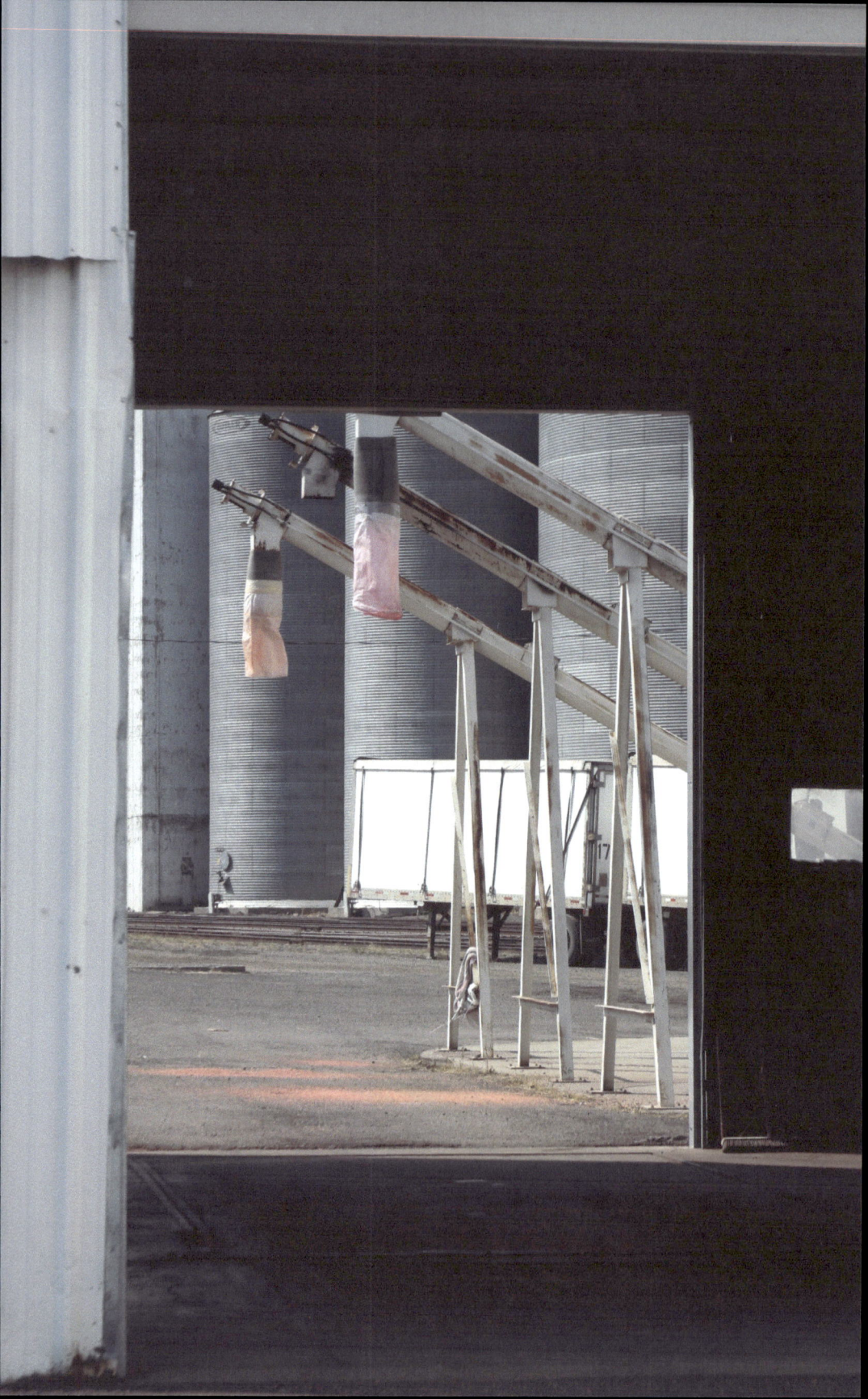

All the crocodiles slithered out of view as Little Gibbon waded to the island. Little Gibbon splashed onto shore, smiled, and lay down for a nap.

He was just starting to fall asleep when he remembered that he had left his house to have an adventure, not to take naps. He could sleep anytime.

Little Gibbon hopped up. He saw his canoe floating peacefully a little ways away. It was dented from crashing down Big Bumpy Falls, but intact.

Little Gibbon waded out to the canoe, got in and fell asleep. He didn't mean to fall asleep, but he did. It was time for his nap.

Big River thought Little Gibbon had had enough adventures for one day. So Big River didn't wake Little Gibbon while he carried the canoe safely down the length of the Island Overrun With Crocodiles.

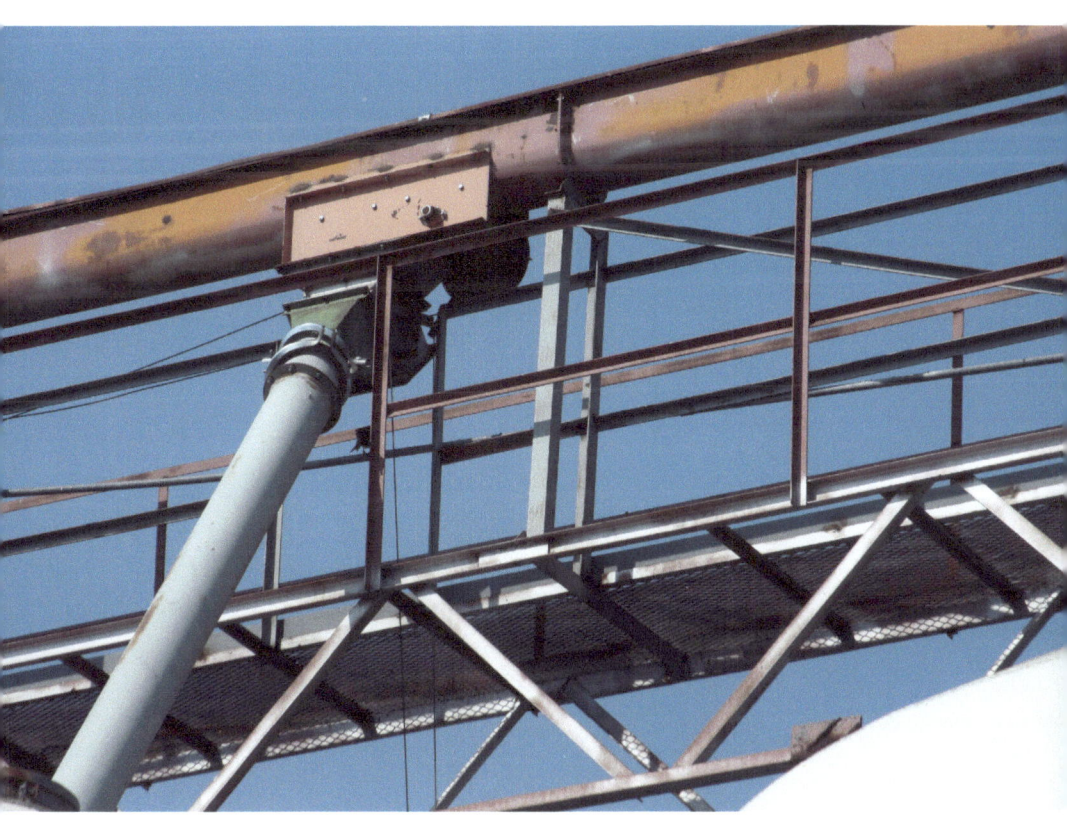

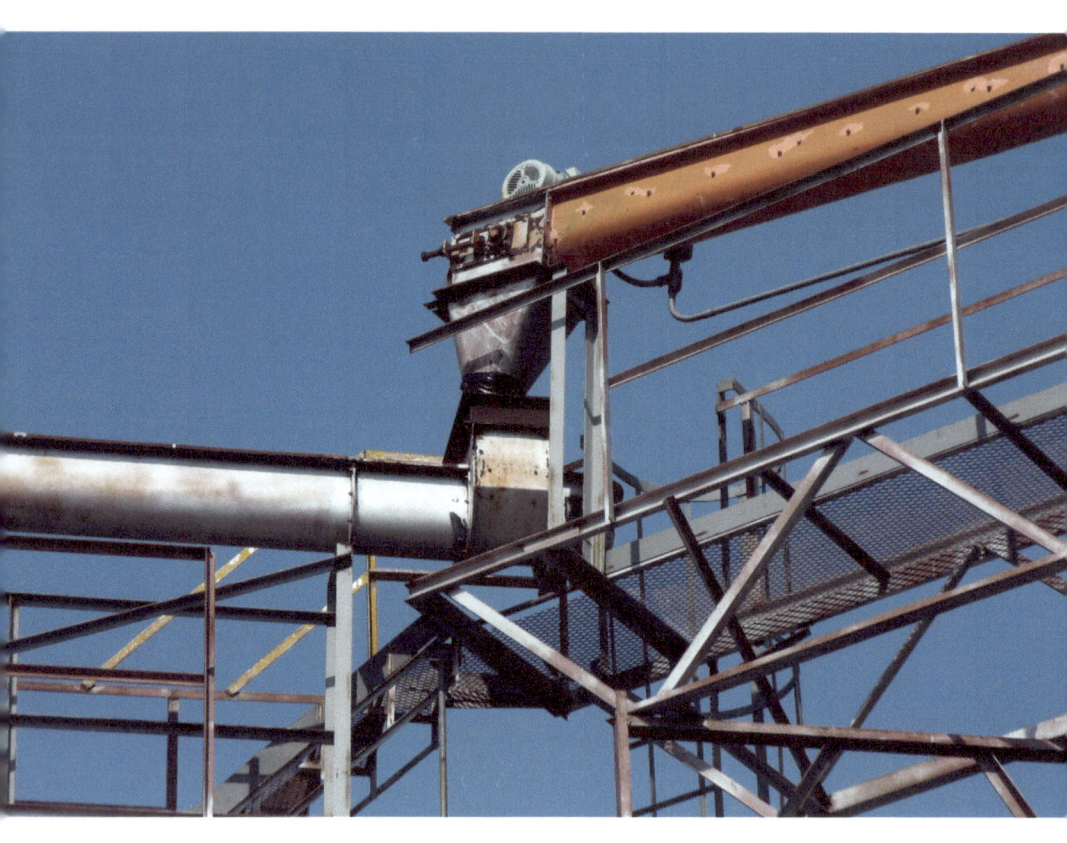

Big River didn't wake Little Gibbon when he gently carried the canoe past the Swamp Of Fierce Snakes.

Big River didn't wake Little Gibbon when he gently carried the canoe past the Hillside Of Snarling Wolves.

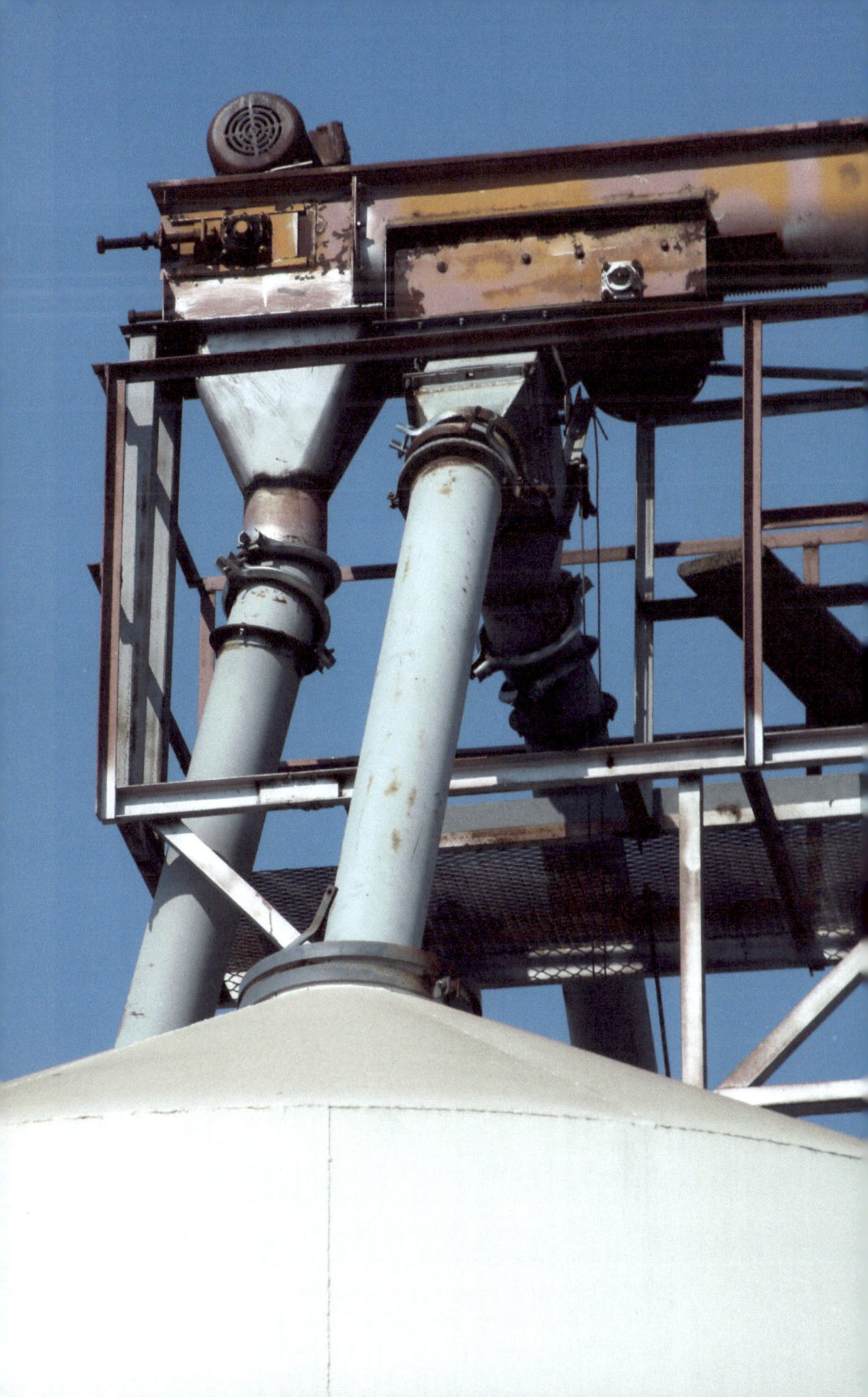

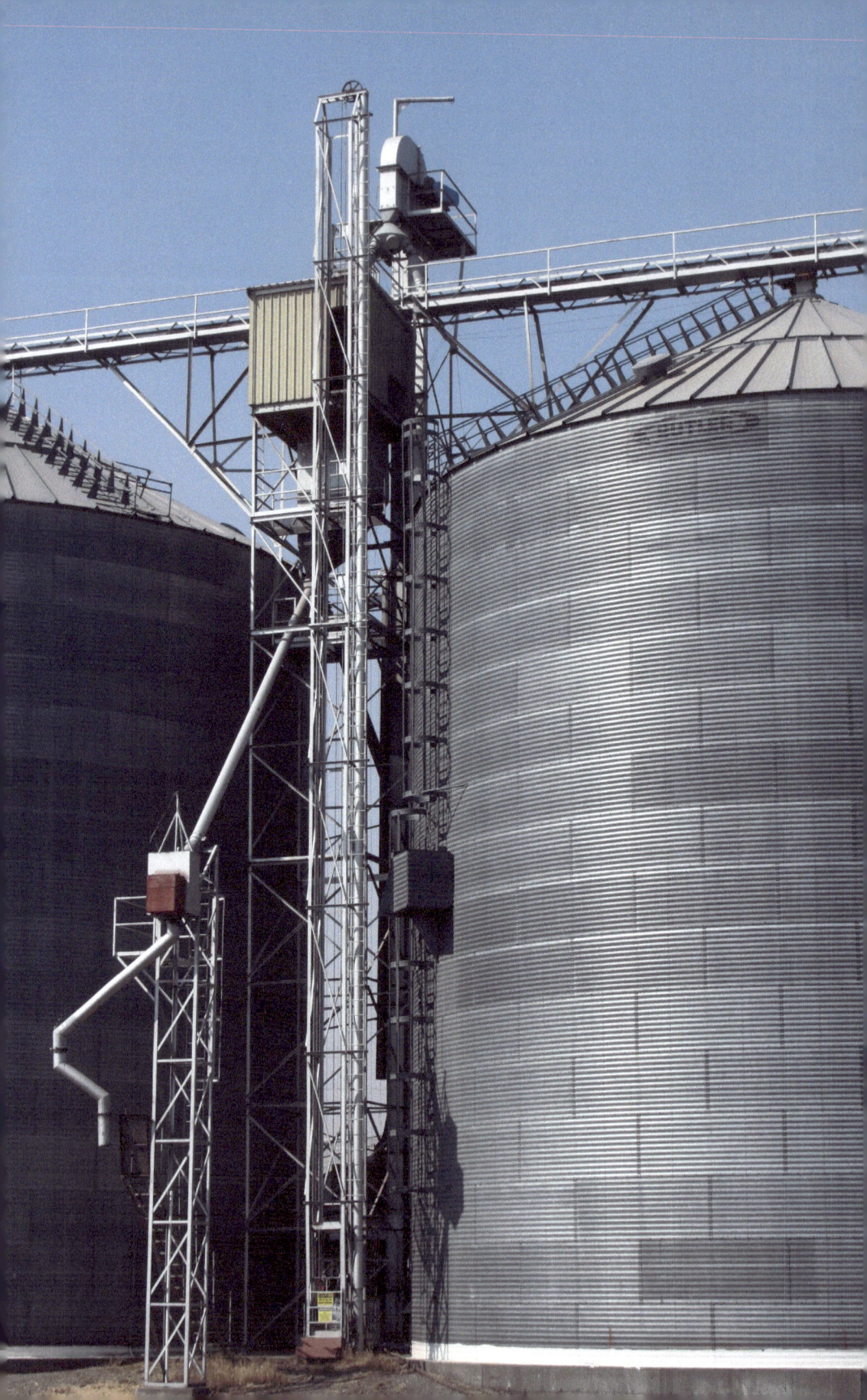

Big River didn't wake Little Gibbon when he gently carried the canoe past the City Of Insane Honking Traffic.

Big River gently carried the canoe all the way to Big Ocean.

Little Gibbon had had enough adventures for one day, thought Big River. There was always tomorrow.

~~

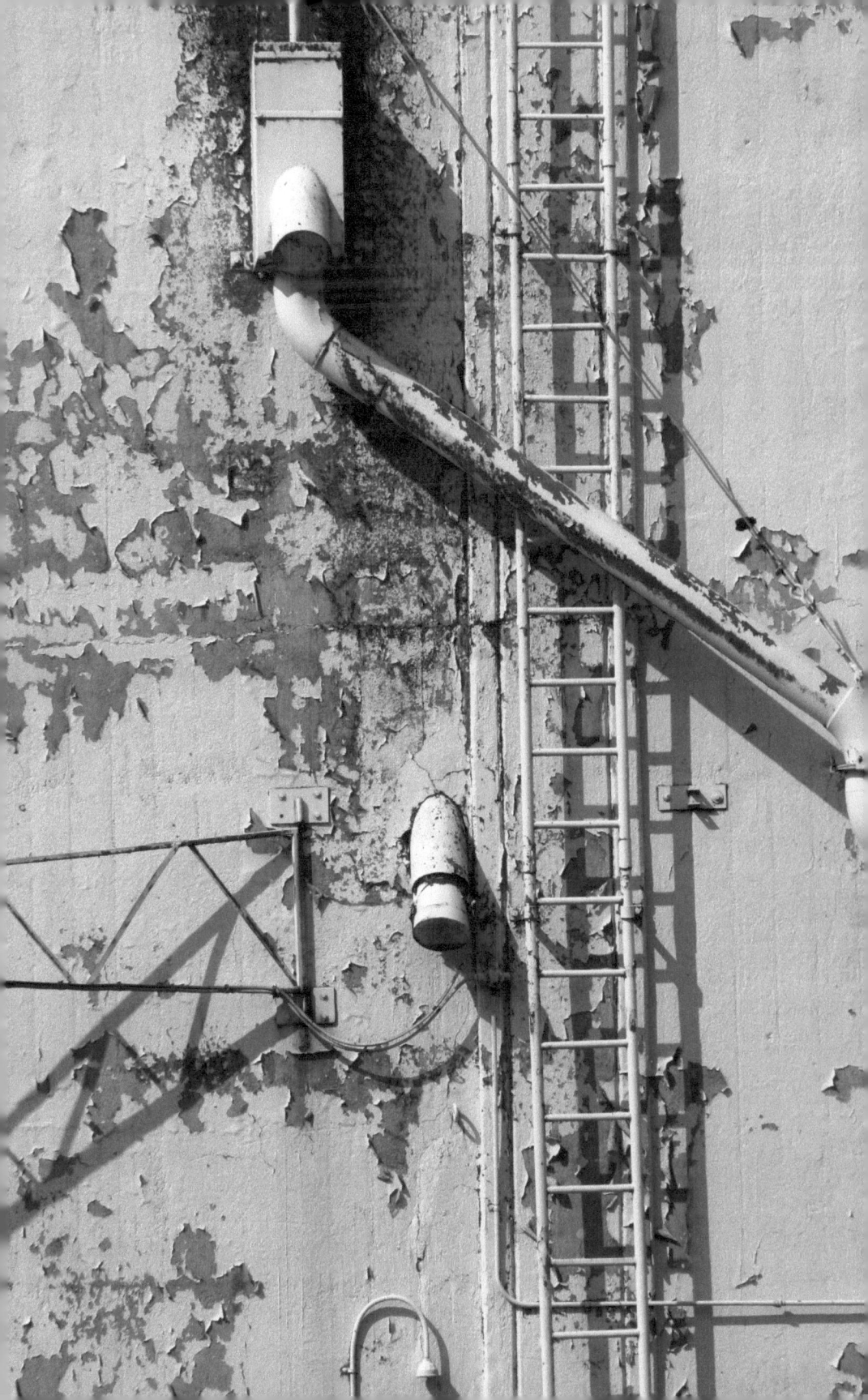

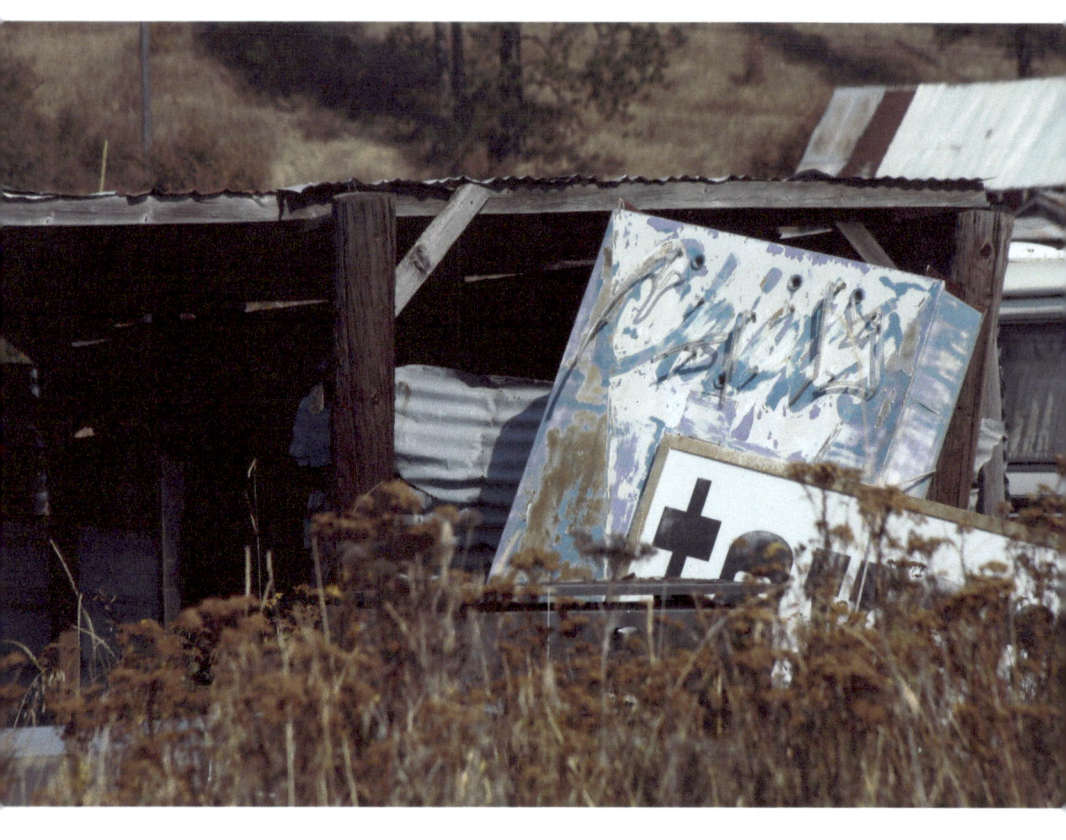

Reflection questions

What adventures do *you* want to have?

What might you need to bring with you on those adventures?

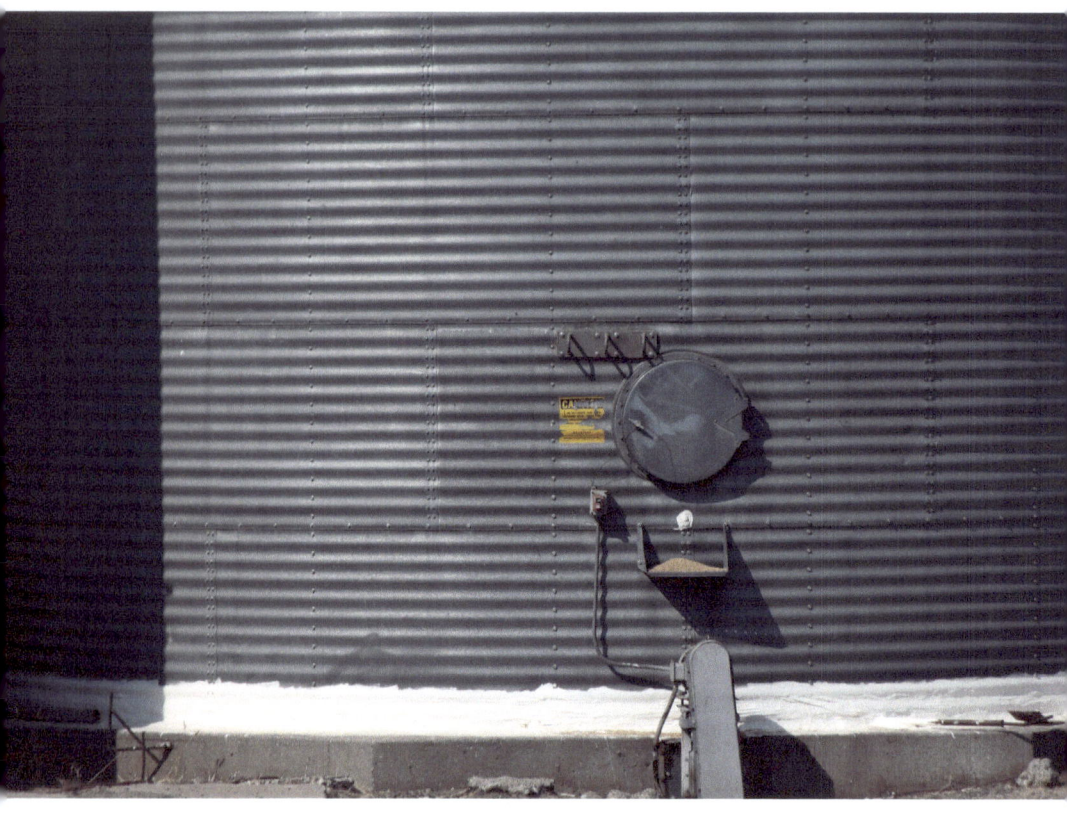

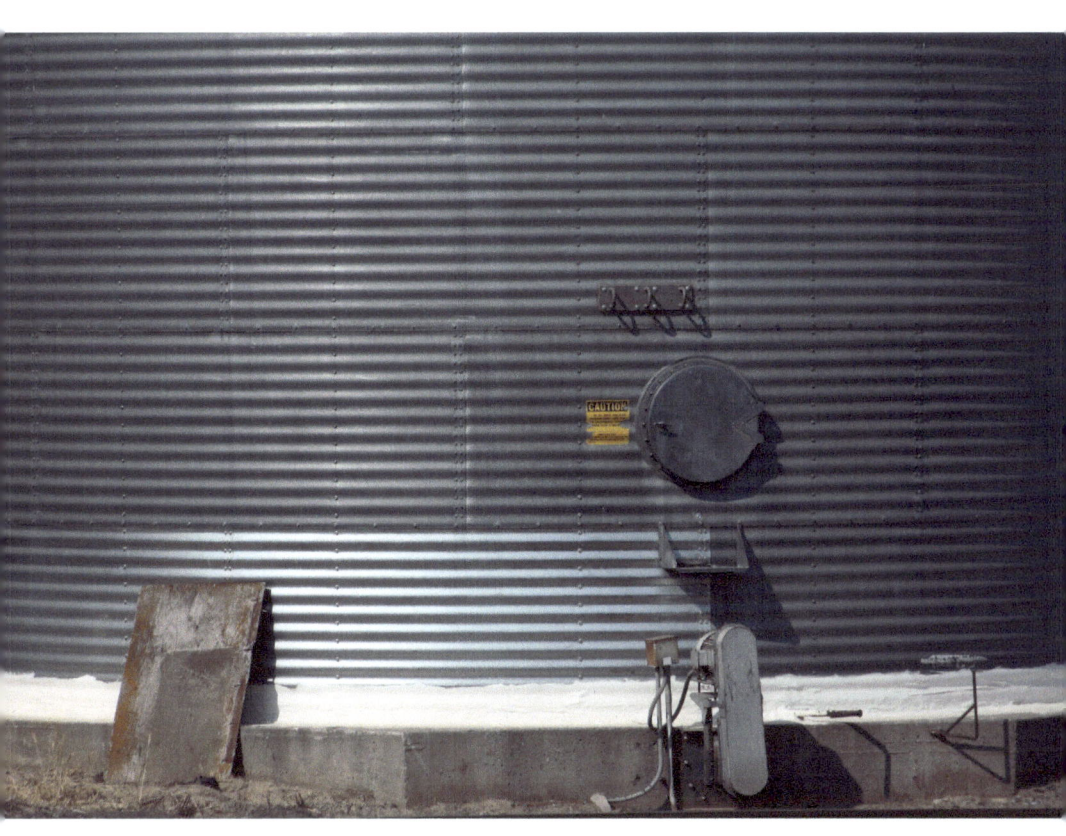

A Mark Dahle Portfolio

Monkey Brains On Big Ocean

Little Gibbon's Big Adventures #2

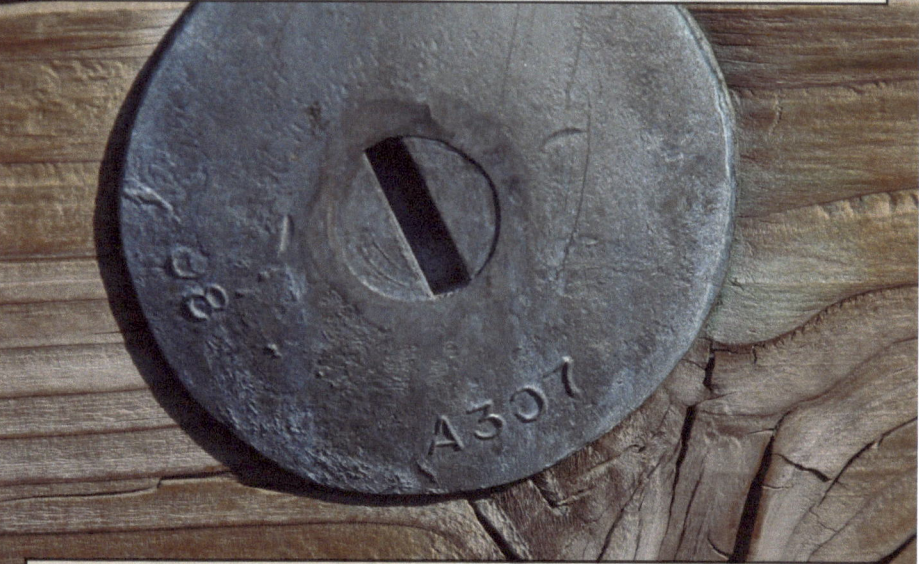

This Mark Dahle Portfolio includes a photo of a colorful abstract painting, twenty-six outstanding photographs from Spokane, Washington, and a story about a gibbon who liked adventures.

Suddenly a tall cliff burst into view, jumping out of the fog. It was cutting through the water, with a wake on each side of it.

Little Gibbon looked up. Way up. He gasped. It was not a cliff. It was a ship. It was enormous, and it was coming straight towards him.

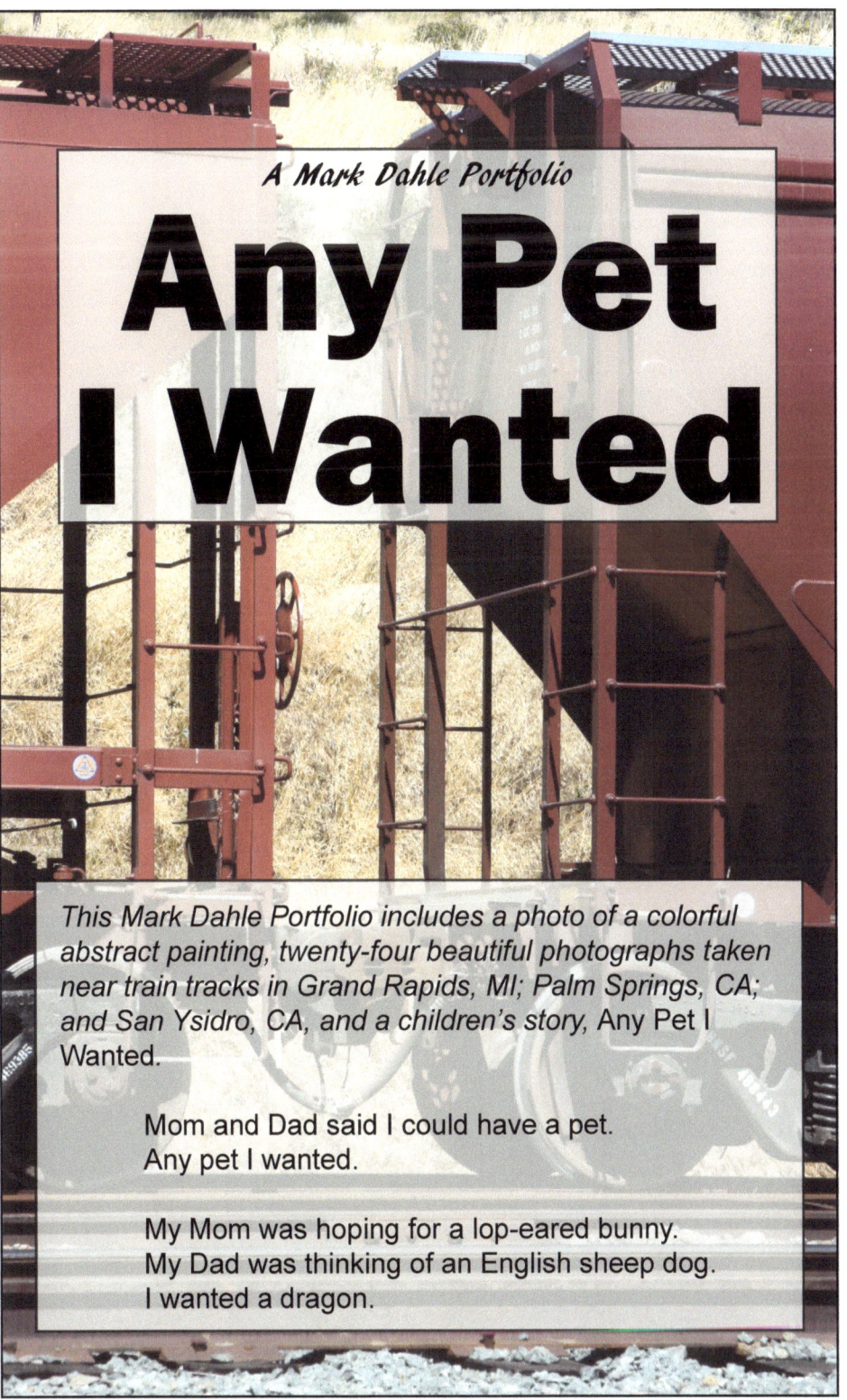

A Mark Dahle Portfolio

Any Pet I Wanted

This Mark Dahle Portfolio includes a photo of a colorful abstract painting, twenty-four beautiful photographs taken near train tracks in Grand Rapids, MI; Palm Springs, CA; and San Ysidro, CA, and a children's story, Any Pet I Wanted.

Mom and Dad said I could have a pet.
Any pet I wanted.

My Mom was hoping for a lop-eared bunny.
My Dad was thinking of an English sheep dog.
I wanted a dragon.

This Mark Dahle Portfolio includes a colorful painting, twenty-six beautiful photographs from Detroit, and a story about a carpenter who made fine furniture from scraps.

The carpenter came across the twig one day while scouring the countryside for debris. He had already found a sheet of plastic, a broken piece of plywood and several rusty, bent nails. Those he knew he could use. But the twig? He could not imagine a use for it. Nevertheless, it caught his attention as he walked along the edge of a forest. He absentmindedly picked it up.

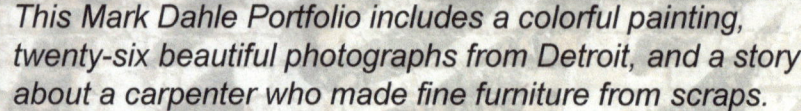

A Mark Dahle Portfolio

The
Carpenter
And
The Twig

www.ingramcontent.com/pod-product-compliance
Lightning Source LLC
Chambersburg PA
CBHW040901180526
45159CB00001B/482